Golf Betting

A Beginner's Guide

By Todd Bishop

Timely Publishing

Table of Contents

Introduction
Setting-Up and the Basic Swing
Days 1-7: Tee Shots
Days 8-14: Approach Shots
Days 15-21: Hitting Mid Irons
Days 21-28: Putting
Conclusion
Copyright

Introduction

Golf is easily one of the most popular and enjoyable sports played by men, women, and children of all ages and backgrounds. That being said it is also one of the more difficult sports to truly master. The art of a great golf swing is complex mechanically and is extremely challenging to perfect.

The golf industry sees revenue in the billions for products that (courses, training material, golf aids) claim to help you get better at golf – providing a shortcut to making you a better golfer. While many of these aids and programs may help to improve your game on a rudimentary level until the essential golf swings are mastered your total game will suffer.

This eBook will take us through the many different swings in golf, offering actionable advice that will help you improve each faucet of your game. And rather than inundating you with hundreds of techniques, tips, and tricks we will walk you through four of the main and most important golf shots.

What we ask is that you break down the lessons taught here into four, one week stints where you just focus on one shot per week. This will help alleviate overwhelm and will ensure that you perfect and hone your skills on one shot at a time. In total you should have a much better understanding and feel for these 4 crucial golf shots – taking a total of 4 weeks or 30 days!

By taking these next four weeks and these four golf shots seriously you can improve your golf game within one month.

Setting-Up and the Basic Swing

Set-Up (Address)

One of the most essential things when it comes to hitting a golf ball is setting it up properly, otherwise known as addressing the ball. (Please note that either the terms set-up or address will be used interchangeably through this book to describe this process).

The set-up of the ball is the first step in a process that makes up your golf shot. It is the beginning stage and will have ramifications on the other aspects of your game. Ensuring a good setup will set the stage for a solid and well performed shot.

Keep in mind that the inverse is true – if you don't set-up your shot properly your chances of hitting the ball well diminish greatly. Addressing the ball properly truly is your key to a solid golf shot.

The Grip

Gripping the club in the proper manner is another essential faucet of the game. When you don't give this the care it deserves your swing and the resulting hit can be affected adversely. Not gripping the club properly can lead to hooks and slices in your shot.

If you are not getting the results you want with your shot – it's veering right, left, or all over the place – one of the first places to look is your grip. If your grip is wonky, your shot will be too.

For a good grip you need to hold the club in a neutral fashion – not too hard and not too soft. To check this take a look at your hands when you're holding the club in your normal stance.

For a neutral grip you should likely see two knuckles on the left hand – at the most three. Not more than three knuckles should be visible with a neutral grip. If two or three knuckles are not visible you need to rotate your hands so that two or three knuckles are visible. You should not rotate the club when you do this – only your hands. Keep in mind if using the overlap grip the thumb on your left hand should run down a portion of the clubs shaft.

Another indication of a solid neutral grip is that you should notice a "V" formation on the right hand located in between the thumb and index fingers. The "V" that gets formed needs to be pointed at the shoulder on your right side. If it's not it's important for you to make adjustments until this is the case.

Golfers in general will find that making these easy adjustments can elevate them of the dreaded problems with slices, hooks, and other such difficulties.

Tightness is another issue that many golfers experience with their grip. At most, you should only ever have a grip that would be considered medium strength. Your movement will be restricted during your swing quite a bit if your grip is too strong. While holding the club too loosely could cause a wobbling of the club on impact with the ball which will likely cause the ball to slice.

Later on in the ebook we will go over why it's important to have a pre-shot routine. Many golfers will visually inspect their grip before taking their shot. You should be incorporating this too.

Alignment

Alignment is another crucial element of any golfer's swing, this goes for your first shot off the green, right down to putting close to the hole. It's a common error to not properly align oneself for a shot when addressing the ball. Even a perfect golf swing will not produce the desired result if not properly aligned at the target.

Target selection is the first step in properly aligning yourself for a shot.

The target you choose depends on the shot that you are trying to make. In order to make the best decision on your target you should do it behind the ball. Once a target is chosen, place the club head behind the ball on the ground, and line it up with the target as you go through the next steps in your set-up routine.

When you watch a professional play, you will notice that the great ones go into their set-up stance after having first set the face of the club. This shows us that this is an effective approach and one you need to implement in your own address stance immediately.

You will want to begin your stance by aligning your feet, hips, and shoulders in a line that is just to the left of your target line.

At this point there is likely a chance that you will naturally want to have the face of the club closed. This will almost guarantee a hook as your body and the club face is directly aligned to the target.

Posture

Your posture will be determined by enlisting the proper alignment of several parts of the body, which will be correspondingly adjusted for the type of shot you are attempting.

To have an effective hit having good posture during your set-up is of the utmost importance. Your shot will suffer a great deal if any part of your posture is off – it's really that simple.

The following are the keys to having a golf posture that is proper:

Stance can be thought of as how you position your feet when addressing the ball. Your feet will need to align with your target when attempting most golf shots.

When setting up to make your swing there are typically three stances that are used. You can improve your game dramatically when you learn each stance and when exactly to use them to your advantage.

The Square Stance

When you want to hit a straight shot the square stance is going to be your 'go to' as it is the most common stance in golf. Getting this stance down will make every difference in your overall game and can't be ignored.

To start with this stance you are going to stand so that your feet line up just on the left side of the target. Think of it as if a straight line where drawn from just on the left side of the target all the way to your toes, the three of these points would ultimately connect; the very end of your shoes, the head of the club, and the target.

The Open Stance

The open stance is a slight off shoot of the square stance and is used in certain situations like – when you're stuck in the sand trap or need to make a chip shot. To do it correctly you're going to want to pull your left foot back while keeping your body along with your shoulders square.

This stance will have the effect of causing the ball to fly out to the right – done correctly and deliberately this result is called a draw; when this occurs by accident it's known as a slice.

The Closed Stance

You can think of the closed stance as a sort of twist on the open stance in that instead of moving your left foot back you are moving it forward. This will cause the ball to deliberately hook because of the path of the swing being inside-to-outside.

The Width of Your Stance

Varying between the type of shot you're going to take the width of your stance will play an important role in overall shot quality. Most shots will use a shoulder-width or slightly less than shoulder-width stance. It is unlikely that using a stance more than shoulder-width will yield favorable results.

A simple rule for the distance between your feet (stance width) is easy:
For long clubs use a slightly wider stance.
For shorter clubs use a slightly narrower stance.
Ball Position

The position of the ball will also play an important role in relation to your posture. Fitting the ball to match your posture doesn't really work so you need to set up your posture so that it fits with the ball along with the kind of shot you are attempting.

Put the ball somewhere in the middle in relation to your stance when using a short club. This causes the contact with the ball to occur in a descending fashion which is what you want in this situation.

Alternatively when using long irons and fairway woods you will want to set yourself up so that the golf ball is just left of the center line. What this does is make it so that the ball is slightly nearer your left foot.

Line up the ball in relation to your left heel on shots using one of your drivers or any of the fairway woods that are longer.

Your Head

You'll hear it a lot – "Stop moving your head!" But, this isn't literally true. Some head movement will occur naturally during your golf swing. The trick is to keep it to a minimum and not raise it too much as more than slight movements can actually through your shot off.

Trying to remain perfectly still just doesn't work anyway. When you do this you'll take a lot of the power out of your swing which dwindles its effectiveness. So feel fine about moving your head a little during your swing. However, you will want to make sure that if and when your head does move it still remains behind the ball.

The Basic Golf Swing

Now it's time to crush it! Once you've gotten down how to stand and position yourself it's actually time to hit the ball! The basic golf swing is going to be your new best friend when starting out.

The Takeaway

You will want to have your arms straight as you start to bring your club back. Remember to keep that left arm straight during your swing, and that your right arm can bend at the elbow when it gets to the level of your waist.

At this time it's crucial that you remain on the right swing path when the club is being brought back. And remember to have the club brought back low in relation to the ground and in as smooth a motion as possible.

The Backswing

To make a full golf swing, you will want to bring the club so far back that ideally it is parallel to the ground. If you can't quite do this, do as much as your flexibility will allow.

Depending on different factors (i.e. distance) certain shots are going to require somewhat less than a full swing. In using your judgement you will only bring the club back as far as you deem necessary when taking your shot.

The key to a strong and powerful shot will be when you get to a spot where your own pivot and the shift in weight come together for a clean shot.

You will also need to try and shift your weight in a relatively smooth manner over to the right when getting into your backswing. Do your best to not sway. And keep your right hip so that it won't end up further than your right foot.

The right and left shoulder will change position with your right moving slightly upward and your left slightly down. You will need to make sure your head stays behind the ball. However, it is alright to allow some horizontal movement.

Your back and hips should move together creating a smooth backswing. Something to keep in mind is preventing your hips from rotating too much. This position and motion should feel natural enough so if it feels at all forced it's likely that you're taking it too far.

Once at the top of the backswing take a moment to pause and then transition effortlessly into the downswing.

The Downswing

The trick to the downswing is actually letting your hips bring you into it. The major and likely problem a golfer will face is letting their hands transition them into the downswing first.

What should start the downswing is a shift in weight that comes from your left hip to your left foot. Again this motion should come to feel natural as things flow from the hips then to the shoulders, to the arms, and then the club. This motion is important in order to build up the right club speed needed for those long fairway shots and drives.

The Follow-Through

The art of the follow-through is sometimes an underrated and undervalued tool in your golf game. Having a solid follow-through will help improve your game on any shot you take – from your short game to your long game.

The key to a good follow-through is to almost continue with the shot after you've hit the ball. You will want your hips to keep pivoting as your arms and shoulders follow along naturally. When making a complete swing, it's important that your eyes, shoulders, chest, and hips to be pointed at the target.

Locking down your follow-through is a crucial part of your game and is something that should not be overlooked.

Having covered a lot of the basics, let's dive into our 30-day program for better golf!

Days 1-7: Tee Shots

If we're honest about it we know that most golfers love driving the ball. It's not only fun but very exhilarating and rewarding. Aside from those great attributes, whenever we deliver a really good shot - it's a beautiful thing.

However, for so many golfers it's the 'Tee Shot' that gives them the most trouble. From hooks to slices to shanks, every golfer is fully aware of what could and many times does go wrong. This section of the article is specifically written to help you correct these problems.

Not every Tee Shot is performed using the driver. Every hole requires a specific club and that fact makes proper club selection all the more important.

The Very First Thing to Do

Purchase a small notebook you can carry in your golf bag. It is literally impossible to gauge which club is the right club for any hole without first knowing the distance you can hit with each of your clubs. On the notebook write down every club you carry, beginning with the driver and moving down to the wedges.

Week 1 Weekly Task #1

During week #1 you should make the effort to visit your choice of driving range no less than one time. However, a couple of times or more is more preferable if you can 'swing it' (pardon the pun).

You start with the shorter clubs, hitting several balls using each of them. You want to write down the average distances in the notebook you put into your bag. Work up to your driver but take your time (you want your averages to be as accurate as you can get them). The information you glean from this exercise will prove to be invaluable later on.

As you are going through your clubs make a note of how you actually hit each one. It could be that you're having some trouble with one particular club while you find another really makes your more comfortable. Write down the clubs and make specific notes about any problems you see.

Tee Shot Basics

Any golfer who has been struggling with his/her game needs to stay focused mainly on keeping their ball in play when they hit from the Tee. Everybody loves distance, even more so off the Tee. However, when you're first beginning accuracy is king.

As you're stepping onto the Tee area, stop for a few seconds and look far down the fairway. Locate a target that is within your capabilities of hitting. Take the distance information you gathered from your visits to the driving range and select the club that best fits in with your chosen target.

When you're setting up, check your grip to ensure you're holding the right posture for your selected club. If it's a driver you're using, make sure your feet are shoulder-length apart, then position your ball slightly off the left heel. Be sure you have your head positioned behind your ball until you make impact.

Regardless of your chosen club for your Tee Shot, don't try to rip through your ball using mostly upper-body strength. This will almost always lead to you making a poor shot. Instead you want to use a very smooth and deliberate stroke that will create good club-head speed. This is the key point in achieving excellent distance.

Days 8-14: Approach Shots

Now that your notebook contains accurate distance readings you should experience easier approach shots in certain respects. One very troubling issues for a lot of golfers who are on the fairway is distance. Many times, their club selection will be based more on guesswork than accurate facts.

In terms of fairway distance there are 2 main issues that everybody faces -

1. How Far Can I Hit With Each of My Clubs?
2. How Far Away Am I From The Target?

Fortunately, one of these questions has already been answered within your notes.

Distance Judging

If you are still struggling when it comes to judging distances then you simply need to improve in this specific area. If you can, you should purchase or maybe borrow a range finder. This will assist you in becoming a better judge of fairway distances.

It's crucial that you become 'better than average' at estimating distances with a high degree of accuracy. For example, let's suppose you're approximately 200 yards off the green. You know from reading your notes that you have a specific club that will make that an easy shot for you. So you pull out that club and hit the ball in good form. However, the ball pulls up well short of the green.

You first thought will be, "Man, my swing is really off!" Then you consider the notion that perhaps you pulled out the wrong club. Finally you find out the reality of the situation - you mistakenly believed your distance was 200 yards and it was actually 220.

In a scenario such as this, rather than recognizing that your problem was a poor judgment of distance, you may blame it on your club selection or your swing. This is where things can become very confusing and even more problems can arise.

Tips to Improve Your Distance Reading Accuracy

When it comes to your approach shots you simply must become an accurate and effective distance reader. The following tips will help you to maximize your efforts whenever you find yourself between 100 & 200 yards off the green:

If you think you're able to reach the green then locate the pin. This is extremely important, especially if the green contains a lot of break or if a bunker is close-by to the pin location.

When you choose a club for this shot, allow for taking a 'full' swing instead of a 'fractional' swing. A Golfer who has a well-practiced swing will usually make better contact using a full swing.

Another thing, the more distance you have between the green and yourself, the more you need to try landing on its center or at its widest section. At the bare minimum you want to wind up on the green.

Prior to making your shot, give yourself some time to evaluate the conditions of the greens. A hard and dry green will cause your ball to run fast and long. Wet or damp greens can restrict the ball from rolling very much at all. So plan your landing target based on how you believe the green will roll your ball.

One last thing before you choose your club - Check the Wind. It could be that you need to add a club or drop one in accordance with the direction and force of the wind.

Hitting Long Irons Correctly

When you know how to hit long irons correctly, it can save you a lot of holes. This is especially true when you're playing on courses that carry several par 5s. There are a few specific things to keep in mind while you play your long irons like -

(1). Solid Iron Shots Always Require Maintaining Your Balance Throughout.
(2). You Want to Make a Swing That's Smooth, Not Too Fast, Not Too Slow.
(3). If You Want Your Shot to be Successful, It's Crucial That You Accelerate Your Club Head All The Way Through to Impact With Your Ball.
(4). Choose Your Target Carefully

Putting Confidence Into Your Swing

Everyone knows how unforgiving long irons can be. The impact on your ball has to be very clean and made with the sweet spot of your club face. Before you play your long iron, make sure you are in a firm stance. This will be crucial to holding your balance properly.

As you're bringing your club back, be sure your tempo matches your type of swing. As you transition from your back-swing to your down-swing you want it to be smooth. It should never be jerky at the top. By maintaining the proper tempo you'll be better able to keep your club face square, which will enable you to pick up speed as you're approaching impact.

Your hands should never be given the lead when you're at the top of your back-swing. You should let the hips begin the process. Doing this will increase your power and add to your distance.

One of the most common mistakes Golfers make when playing their long irons is to lift their head too soon to keep their eye on the ball. This mistake can cause your club to strike the ground prior to connecting with the ball. The end result is a poor shot. You should focus on keeping your head down and resist the urge to lift it.

Another very common mistake is attempting to lift your ball off the ground using the club face. Anytime you're playing long irons you need to hit your ball first and the ground second. This requires a crisp, downward stroke.

With any golf shot you never want to stop your follow-through too soon. Allow your hips to rotate fully and finish with your hands up high and your torso facing the target.

How to Properly Hit Fairway Woods

You need to reach a place of confidence and competency when hitting fairway woods. Golfers who struggle in this area will often just leave them in their bag even if they need them. This can cost strokes and detract from self-confidence.

One of the primary keys in becoming a better Golfer in just 30 days, is learning the difference between each club in your bag. Hitting woods off the fairway is different from hitting long irons.

The following are some tips for maximizing your skills using fairway woods

When setting up with your wood, place your feet in a positional 'square' stance. The only exception to this rule is when you're deliberately trying to hit a draw or fade. In these cases you should place your feet shoulder-width apart.

With most Golf shots you should play the ball forward from your stance. For the majority of players that means off the left foot. Maintain arm extension and never slouch over your ball. Bend at the knees slightly to help improve your balance.

For hitting a solid wood shot you must keep your forward arm as straight as you possibly can. It's also very important to pivot your hips throughout your back-swing and down-swing. Make sure your head stays behind your ball at all times. That will gain you the most power from your swing.

Remember, it's crucial that you don't try lifting your ball using the club head. You want to hit your ball cleanly and leave as small a divot as possible, if any.

When you try to rip your ball to gain distance when using fairway woods, it can lead to a shank or a wild shot. You need to learn to trust in your swing! All it takes is a smooth swing to get your ball off the ground and headed down the fairway.

Week 2 Weekly Task #1

There aren't many recreational Golfers who spend very much time practicing to improve their fairway wood skills. That gives you an opportunity to get ahead of the pack by visiting your driving range and practicing with your long irons and fairway woods. Work with each of them until you feel comfortable using them all. Don't use a rubber tee on your mat. Play your club as if you are on the course. Keep good notes on the distances you're able to achieve.

Days 15-21: Hitting Mid Irons

Your mid-irons (5,6,7) are considered to be the work-horses of your bag. That's because on most days Golfers make a lot of shots with these particular clubs. The reason is their versatility and the fact that they are easier to master.

If you're experiencing trouble using mid-irons, take some time and look over your basic setup. Keep in mind that the shorter your club is the narrower the stance you'll need to take. If you play these clubs placing your feet too wide apart it can lead to bad hits. That's because your stance will affect where your club head will impact your ball.

When playing mid-irons you should let your shoulders dominate your swing. Let your arms and hands follow your swing and not lead. The arc of your swing needs to be more insider the line when you use these clubs, even more so than the other clubs you have in your bag.

While you are in your back-swing your wrists cock naturally. That puts your club on its desired vertical level. As your weight is shifting, keep your right elbow close to the body. Upon reaching the top of the swing, 90% of your weight needs to be on the right side of your body. Let your hips start your down-swing and you'll find that the arms and hands will follow.

Week 3 Weekly Task #1

If you struggle to master your mid-irons, take them out to the backyard or to the range and practice. Do not just hit your ball. Take the time to learn the proper foot width, ball position, and stance for your body. Once you've learned the right positions then head out to the range and hit a few balls. Keep track of the distance achievements by writing them in your notebook.

The Short Game

A lot of Golfers believe that the short game is among the most vital components in being a successful Golfer. There are several shots that make up the short game like pitching, chipping, and putting. Of course putting is a huge component for all holes.

It's highly unlikely that any Golfer will master all aspects of their short game without investing a lot of time using their clubs. However, by honing your short game skills you have a much better chance of shaving strokes of your score card. If you need more proof of that you can ask Phil Mickelson.

Your Short Game Starts With Your Short Irons (8 & 9)

You can use the 8 and 9 irons for a broad range of shots. They're very effective when you need a loft and some distance. They are also used many times to replace various wedge shots. They're not only effective when you're working close to the green, they're also needed for playing a lot of Par 3 Tee Shots.

An important point about these clubs is that they're very versatile. That means every single shot and every lie is going to call for its own unique setup and stance. Your wedges and short irons are the 2 best clubs you have for experimenting. They allow you to adjust your grip, ball position, and stance, so you can learn to make shots just like the pros.

Even though the short irons are among the easiest to use, many Golfers still mistakenly try to get way too much distance from them by ripping through their ball using their arms. Over and over again this will only lead to bad shots.

Instead of slamming your ball using muscular force try to use more club. That will ensure you make a smooth swing. For lots of Golfers this one tip alone will save them 2 or 3 strokes per round.

When using your short irons you should always remember to hit your ball using a downward arc. Then you accelerate your club head at point of contact with your ball by utilizing the proper stance.

Chipping

There are some newer Golfers who confuse 'chipping' and 'pitching'. The difference is that chipping is more similar to putting. A chipping swing is more restricted to just the shoulders and arms. Your body remains still.

What makes a good chip shot is a proper setup and swing. Whenever you set up to make a chip shot you need to use an 'open stance'. Keep your feet and hips opened slightly toward your target. It's natural for this stance to feel a bit odd at first. However, it's necessary for giving your arms the room they need to swing through your target. When you make a chip shot and use a square stance, your wrists are at risk of unhinging.

Play your ball toward the back foot while narrowing your stance. Utilize a neutral grip but keep the shaft lined up with the left thigh. You might even move your hands down more on the shaft to give yourself better control.

Now, using your shoulders, execute a basic pendulum swing. Be sure you hit your ball first and then the ground.

Different Types of Chips

You have 3 basic chip types and each one has its own unique purpose. If you can learn to perform all 3 well, it will greatly increase your Golfing abilities. The types are -

(1). Standard Chip Shot

The goal with this chip shot is getting the ball airborne for around 1/3rd of the way to the hole and letting it roll to the hole from there.

Most Golfers prefer a 9-iron or wedge for this shot. You should keep your feet pretty close together. You want to play your ball in the center of your stance. You should keep your hands well ahead of your ball so you connect properly. While making your pendulum swing make sure you keep your club face square.

(2). The Soft Chip

This chip enables your ball to stay airborne longer. When it hits the green it should stop fairly quick. Most players like a lob wedge or sand wedge for this one.

Unlike the previous 'standard chip' this one requires that you open your club face a little. You'll play your ball forward in your stance while keeping your feet close together and your hands ahead of your ball through to impact.

For this specific shot you'll want to accelerate your club head on your down-swing. However, be careful that you don't accelerate 'too much'.

(3). Low Ball Chip

This one is really good to have as part of your arsenal, especially when there's lots of distance to cover once you're on the green. Usually the low ball chip is performed using one of your mid-irons. When setting up and getting into your stance, play your ball to the back of it. Be sure to hit your ball using a downward arc. You need to keep your hands in front of your club head while you swing. You also want to keep the face square to your target.

A low ball chip allows a lot of roll after your ball hits on the green. An accurate aim is crucial to sinking your ball using this chip shot.

Week 3 Weekly Task #2

Give yourself a couple of hours learning about various chip shots. To learn to gauge how much roll you're getting with your shots, it's best to practice these at a practice green.

Pitching

The difference between chipping and pitching is that pitching involves some body pivot. It's perfect for shots that are from 50 to 100 yards from the green.

You need a lofted club to shoot a good pitch shot. Most Golfers like the wedges but will often choose a 6 or 7-iron depending on the distance. Similar to chipping, pitching also require a proper setup and swing before it will be effective.

Address your ball with an open stance. Keep your feet aimed a bit to the left of the target. As you start your swing, keep more of your weight on the left foot than the right. Your back-swing needs to be smooth and well adjusted to suit the distance. Most back-swings on pitch shots stop either at shoulder or waist level.

Make sure your head is behind your ball with your hands ahead of your club. You should impact your ball using a downward arc while keeping your club face square. The follow-through might not end high but should extend enough to let your hips rotate all the way through.

Week 3 Weekly Task #3

Try to spend a couple of hours practicing on your pitch shot. Try using a variety of clubs and take notes on how each club behaves.

Tips For Pitching & Chipping From The Rough

Knowing how to chip and pitch can work absolute miracles if you wind up with your ball in the rough. Playing a chip or pitch from the rough differs some from playing shots off the fairway.

Here are some common examples to show where you may need to chip or pitch out of the rough and how to have success with it:

Playing From Tall Grass When You're Close to The Green

If you're in tall grass and close to the green pull out your sand wedge or lob wedge. Address your ball with the hips with your feet positioned in an open stance and fairly close together. Put most of your weight onto the left foot.

These 2 things are key - Be sure to position your hands properly by lining them up with your left thigh. You also want to choke downward on the shaft to gain better control.

When you're beginning your back-swing you should let the shoulders turn while cocking your wrists. The club head needs to come upward at a steep angle.

For your down-swing you want to rotate the hips smoothly and let your arms follow. Strike your ball like you're trying to trap it in between the face of your club and the ground. When this is done properly your ball will pop up out of the tall grass.

A Low Flight Path From a Medium Rough

Whenever you are need of a pitch or chip from a medium rough and at the same time need a considerable rolling distance, use a low ball shot. This one is best accomplished using a sand wedge.

Your setup is the same as the previous one. Play your ball off the back foot while keeping the hands ahead of your club as you strike your ball. A lot of Golfers miss this shot because of improper hand position when the club impacts the ball. Keep your hands forward!

Moving into the follow-through your club is positioned on a low plane and pointing toward your target.

To Get Less Roll Use a High Ball

Whenever you need to get across an obstacle without your ball rolling too much when it lands, your best choice of club for performing this type of shot is the lob wedge.

If you're shooting this shot from the rough you need to keep your ball positioned in the center of your stance. Your lob wedge shaft needs to barely lean toward your target line.

Moving downward into the down-swing you want to keep the hands well ahead of your club. That is a crucial key for performing this shot with success. Coming through impact make sure the arms are extended as well as pointed at your target.

Keep in mind that your target should be where you want the ball to land. The hole is not the target!

Playing Out of Sand Traps

Those who have Golfed long enough understand that you will inevitably be landing in a sand trap at some time or another. Fortunately, getting out of one isn't as complicated as some people believe.

You begin by sizing up all your options. If the ball sits on top of the sand, with not big side slopes ahead of you, it might be good to try a normal shot aimed directly at the green.

If the ball is buried or you're unable to breach the bunker's side easily, you might want to think about playing it safe.

Now for club selection. There is no hard and fast rule saying you MUST use a sand wedge when you're in a sand trap. There are Golfers who like playing a wood out of traps.

The large majority of sand shots require a stance designed slightly open to the target. You should wiggle your feet and firmly plant them into the sand. Now choke down ever so slightly on the club. Your ball is usually played off your left foot but can be adjusted as needed.

Whenever you're ready to take your swing, bring the club back as far as necessary to hit your ball. To have a successful down-swing you'll have to accelerate your club head while making contact with your ball.

Be sure your club enters the sand at least 1 or maybe 2 inches behind your ball. Allow your club to do all the work while it enters the sand. Avoid trying to scoop your ball upward and out.

A crucial element of all sand shots is to 'accelerate through impact'. This is especially true when the sand is wet or packed tightly. The acceleration will be the one single thing keeping the club head from stopping as it impacts its way through the sand.

A sand shot follow-through has to be full as well as smooth without any sudden stops. Keep the head down and avoid the urge to eye the ball as it's coming out.

Week 3 Weekly Task #3

Be sure to spend some time practicing greens and sand areas. Try out different clubs and vary the depth of the ball from up on top to almost buried. That's the way you master your sand play.

Days 21-28: Putting

There are no Golfing components that steal more strokes than putting. A player will lose more strokes putting on the green than literally anywhere else. It may surprise you to learn that more than 40% of all strokes you'll make in a normal round will happen on the green!

So a serious Golfer wanting to improve their game and lower their score will stay focused on their putting.

Putting Mechanics

No golf shot you'll ever attempt is more unique than putting. It's literally impossible to offer you universal tips that are going to work for everyone. However, there are a few common factors that can be applied to everyone for improving their putting.

Just like with other shots the grip on your putter needs to be neutral. If you open or close your putter face it leads to missed putts.

Having a good balance is crucial to putting well. It's perfectly fine to utilize a variety of stances providing the one your select gives you the following -

1. Solid Footing.
2. Doesn't Cause You to Sway (any direction).
3. Enables You to Look Down Directly Over Your Ball as You Putt.

You also don't want to position your head too far behind your ball or too far ahead.

Some players like putting with their arms straight while others like keeping their arms bent. Select whatever position works best and is comfortable for you. Use it consistently throughout your putting stroke.

This shot can be played off either foot or even somewhere in between. Many professionals tend to play their ball more toward the inside off the left foot.

Putting Stroke

Always resist the urge to 'over-think' a putting stroke. It's basically a simple pendulum movement using your shoulders and arms. The hands are simply holding your putter and doing nothing else. The hips and legs shouldn't move at all.

When you putt you should place your weight evenly on both feet and not shift to either side as you stroke.

It's also important that you keep your head down and keep it there until long after hitting the ball. If you move your head too soon it can cause your putter face to go out of its square alignment.

Reading a Green

Learning to read greens can only be done by doing it. There's no written material that can out-perform good old experience. In order to properly read a green you must be able to assess a break if one exists.

Squat down behind the ball and get a view from the ball to the cup. Try to see any slopes existing between your ball and the cup. If there is, you'll have to compensate for it by strategizing your target path.

Remember that the slower your ball moves the more it's going to break toward the downside of the slope.

Also check out the grain of the grass. When hitting 'into' the grain your ball will be traveling slower and breaking more. If putting into a side-grain your ball well tend to move downside along with the grain (aim a bit higher to compensate).

Another good way of improving your putting is learning how to hit your ball harder when you need to. A lot of golfers tend to shy away from doing this. They end up with their breaking putts falling way too short off the downside of the hole.

Your ball has to be hit hard enough to make it roll along the slope and ride it until it finds the side of the hole and falls in.

Anytime you're reading a green and checking for breaks, you want to do it from all angles. Look from the left, the right, the front, and the rear. The more thoroughly you scan the green the more information you'll obtain. Once you get the hang of this you'll be able to do in in just a few seconds.

There's only one good way of mastering this skill and that's spending time practicing on the green. Read putt after putt and you'll see your performance improve. Experience is your only ally when it comes to reading breaking putts.

Distance Control

The goal of distance control is simply to get your ball either to the hole or close as you possibly can. It consists of 2 main elements -

(1). Length of Your Putt
(2). Speed of The Green

and it is both a science and an art. Many times it's a matter of 'feel'. Begin by looking at it to judge how far your ball is away from the cup. As you become more experienced you'll get a sense for judging how hard you should hit your ball to get it to the cup. However, you always have to consider the speed of that particular green.

There are many factors involved in determining green speed. You have these things to consider -

(a). Grain of The Grass.
(b). Dampness/Dryness Level.
(c). The Slope.

Tips for Improving Your Distance Control

There's absolutely NO substitute for practice. Becoming proficient at controlling your distance means consistently hitting balls from various lengths and across various lies. When you're performing these drills don't concentrate on sinking the putt, stay focused on distance only.

While practicing you should be moving around the green. Try to experience putting from as many lies as you can. Read each putt carefully while paying close attention to your results. Don't let yourself become discouraged because it takes 'everyone' some time to master this skill.

One of the major mistakes a lot of Golfers make when they're facing a long putt, is using their wrists like hinges to add power to their stroke. Many times that will cause the putter face to open or close and throw the ball off the target line.

The best option in this case would be to employ a longer stroke. You should bring your putter farther back and gain the added power you need.

Always avoid a fast stroke. Some players think swinging their putter faster than usual gives them more distance. Stick with the longer stroke instead.

As with any Golf shot the putt requires having a good follow-through. Your head should remain down well past impact, letting your putter move forward at about the same length you brought it back.

Conclusion

If you have a solid commitment and practice regularly you can improve your Golf game in just 30 days. When you break it down into several distinct processes as described above, from the tee shots to putting, you'll be able to address each individual aspect of the game and develop your own unique and invaluable set of skills.

When going through this program as outline within this e-book, it's important that you not only keep track of your strongest areas but your weakest ones too. Then you'll know exactly what to concentrate some extra effort on.

I've heard it said many times that it takes an entire lifetime to truly master this game we call 'Golf'. While that may be true, I believe anyone is capable of honing their Golfing skills within a 30 day period. Out of all the Golfing improvement programs on the market today, working on individuals skill and focusing on them one at a time, is the simplest and most effective by far.

You can take this information and start out on your own path of improved Golf play today. In a matter of a few days you'll begin to see the positive results.

Copyright

Copyright ©2017 by Timely Publishing

All rights reserved. No part of this book may be reproduced in any form without permission in writing from the author or publisher.

Disclaimer

The Ideas, concepts and everything else in this book are simply the opinion of the author and the publisher. We hope this book answers some of your questions and provides valuable guidance for you.

As the author and publisher, we make no representations as to the accuracy, completeness, correctness, suitability, or validity of any of the information in this book and will not be liable for any errors, omissions, or delays in this information or any losses, injuries, or damages arising from its display or use. This book is for entertainment purposes only.

All the information provided in this book is on an as-is basis. You are solely responsible for your own choices. There are absolutely no guarantees in this book. Neither the author nor the publisher assume any responsibility or liability whatsoever on the behalf of the purchaser or reader of these materials. Any perceived slight of any individual or organization is purely unintentional.

We sometimes use affiliate links in the content. This means if you decide to make a purchase, we will get a sales commission. But that doesn't mean our opinion is for sale. Every affiliate link is to a product that we feel may be useful given the circumstances. Please do your own research before making any purchase online.

Printed in Great Britain
by Amazon